TRESEDER'S SEEDS

a play for six women

by
Christine Woolf

CHARACTERS

Jane Gifford: A Woman had given birth to an illegitimate baby on her way from work at Wheal Harmony mine. The *West Briton* quotes from the inquest on the dead child "she confessed to having delivered herself near the hedge in Treleigh Lane (near Redruth), and that while doing so she lost her senses and lay upon the child for a considerable time; when she came to herself she found the child was still under her, and she took it in her cloak and apron and carried it home before her ...." She had been brought before the court, but refused to name the father, and had been committed to four years in Bodmin gaol.
On being freed she applied for emigration to work as a maidservant in New Zealand.
The character is based upon the West Briton account, but, like the others, is imaginary.

Elizabeth Blamey: her husband had emigrated seven years previously. He had now acquired land and built a house on it, and has now sent for her to join him. She is taking household goods, sewing kit, various packets of Treseder's seeds, which her husband requires.

Keziah Harding: brought up in workhouse and did not know parents. Taken on to farm for indoor service but often worked in fields. Of them all the poorest.

Mary Ann Webb: emigrating to go into service with a family that has done well, known to her family in Cornwall.

Has the security of knowing she has a job when she reaches Auckland.

Voices of the past:
Margaret: first witness; Mrs. Treseder; Keziah's mistress, Aunt Mag, first Mask.
Martha: second witness; Mrs. Rowe; Mrs. Lean, Aunt Martha, second Mask.

Treseder : It is usual in Cornish 3 syllable names to put the emphasis on the second syllable. However, Treseder is pronounced with the emphasis on the first syllable.

The Union is an abbreviated term for the Union Workhouse.

SETTING

March 1843. The *Westminster* sailed from Plymouth on 4th December 1842, and is nearing the end of its long voyage (118 days). We see dimly the cramped quarters of the six single women emigrants in the stern of the *Westminster*.

UC are wooden screens which surround the area of the women's quarters. Two benches, bales of luggage, bags, blankets are used for sitting and sleeping. Lighting gleams on faces and hands, but is minimal.

Two large Maori-type masks are needed.

Stage L & R are open areas for time slip action, and are lit when required. Action from the women's quarters may also spill on to these areas.

Sound is important. A steady roar, the downward rush of wind through sails, is constant, as is the boom and wash of waves, the rattle of wires and rigging, creaking or wood. Occasionally there are shouted orders to the crew, and bells ringing.

The play moves from the realism of life in the emigrants' quarters to stylised action of the past and future.

The Westminster sailed as stated above. The women whose lives are portrayed in the play are a blend of local newspaper reports of the 1840s, and the writer's imagination. The advertisement for Treseder's Seeds appeared in the *West Briton* newspaper, in early Victorian times.

As the curtain rises, there is blackout, followed by just enough light on central area to see the sleeping forms of the women. Slowly one of them [Keziah] rises, checks that no one is awake, then slips across to take something [packets of seeds] from the baggage belonging to another woman. Silently she returns to hide her booty amongst her own belongings. She does not notice that another woman [Jane] has awoken and is watching her. Throughout this sequence, ship sound at full volume.

BLACKOUT – *10 seconds* – *ship sound continues. Sound gradually dimmed to a whisper.*

Lights up on central area. Early evening of the next day. Elizabeth and Mary-Ann are washing their tin plates and mugs in a bucket , Keziah is sewing. Jane is hacking another notch from timber of ship. She sings to herself, but breaks off when Keziah speaks.

Keziah: How many days now Jane? How many endless days and nights since we left Plymouth?

Jane: A hundred, exactly, for we left on the fourth of December, didn't us?

Keziah: And now 'tis March, I do know that.

1

Jane: And it seems forever since we came aboard the ship; lying out off Cawsand, she were, and the hills of Cornwall behind her, grey and still.

Keziah: And we've never been **still** since. I'll never forget that Bay of Biscay – my stomach heaves at the very name ....

Mary Ann: Psalm 33. "He gathereth the waters of the seas together as an heap."

The ship lurches, depicted by sound up to very loud for 3 seconds. The women stagger. Sound down to whisper.

Jane: The gales – and the swell. The boat tossed up and down fore to stern, and rolling side to side .... The worst was never getting into the fresh air, up on deck.

Keziah: And expecting every moment to be drowned in 'ere, trapped in like a sackful of kittens.

Elizabeth: But we didn't drown, and it got better as we sailed off Africa, you must admit.

Jane: Washing our clothes at last, even if it was only sea water.

Elizabeth: D'you know, I've almost forgotten now what 'tis like to wear really dry clothes, rinsed in good water and dried out on the furze bush, and pressed out and aired by the fire.

Jane, Keziah, Mary Ann: *(remembering)* Oh yes.

Jane and Keziah draw apart from the others.

Jane: You've never told us, Keziah, but you're not from the mining country are you?

Keziah: No, I come from up St. Columb. I never knew my father, nor my mother, come to that. I lived in the union work house till I was thirteen, and then my master and mistress took me away to work for them on their farm. I was supposed to help missus in the kitchen and dairy but as I got older, master would bid me go out to work in the fields.

Jane: That would be some hard.

Keziah: It was. Mud! An' I came to be frightened of the master. He used to stare at me. He never touched me nor nothing, but I came to believe he was only biding his time. Then my mistress must have noticed it too.

Enter Mistress to area DR – Keziah joins her. Lights dimmed in central area. D.R. area spot lit. Ship sound ceases.

Mistress: Keziah.

Keziah: Yes mum?

Mistress: Have you been flaunting yourself before the master?

Keziah: *(frightened)* No mum. I swear to you I haven't.

Mistress: You have become an unsettling presence in this house, Keziah, and so you must go.

Exit Mistress. DR spot out. Keziah turns in to central area again. Lights up centre. Ship sound resumes.

Jane: And where did you go?

Keziah: I worked on farms, for it was all I knew. Sometimes dairy work; usually the fields. For years and years. It's all a blur now, mud and fields and kitchens. But one winter when I was at Trehaven, near to Bodmin, Mrs. Lean taught me how to read. She said I learnt very quick. The missus had the Bible and I read a page every night. And once I could read I knew I could do better.

Enter Mrs. Lean to spot DL. Keziah joins her. Lights dimmed central area. Ship sound ceases.

Mrs. Lean: Well, Keziah, what do you **want** to do?

Keziah: To go away, ma'am, really. Start somewhere fresh like.

Mrs. Lean: I was reading 'bout the emigrants in the West Briton. They go to the new countries. Like New Zealand. Would you like that? It would certainly be a new start. Though I shall miss you, Keziah. You're a good worker.

Keziah: I would like to go ma'am. A new country – fancy.

Mrs Lean: Very well. I'll ask my husband and we'll see what can be done.

Exit Mrs. Lean. Keziah turns in to central area. Lights up centre. Ship sound resumes.

Keziah: And so she found the name of one of the Commissioners and Mr and Mrs Lean stood guarantee for me. Eight guineas they paid for me, out of their own pockets.

Jane: It were very good of them, Keziah, and you must not let them down.

Mary Ann: *That's* done, then. What's to do now? I'm not sleepy. Tisn't right, they cabin passengers can stay up on deck till nine o'clock or later, but us 'emigrants' have to be locked in here by eight. I'll never get used to having a

4

Matron, to lock us in like prisoners! *(She picks up mugs and plates to stow them on the shelf, and trips over Elizabeth's feet as the ship lurches. Sound up briefly. Women stagger. Sound down to whisper)* Ooh, mind yourself. What I'd give to stand on dry, unmoving land, with room to walk about, stead of stumbling round in this black hole.

Jane: We've done a hundred days though, Mary Ann, and Matron says we're making for the Tasman Sea. Think of that.

Mary Ann: We're not far off. Why, you'll be sowing they seeds soon, Elizabeth.

Elizabeth: Yes, so I will. *(She reaches into a bag and takes out the canvas bags and packets of seed).* It won't be long now. *(They gather round, pleased by the sight of the neat packets).* There's oats here, barley, wheat. And here's my vegetables — cabbage and onions — oh, and lettuce. That reminds me. Did I ever tell you 'bout old Mrs. Rowe and her lettuces? Well, she came up to me ...

Enter Mrs. Rowe to spot DL. Elizabeth joins her. Lights dimmed central area. Ship sound ceases.

Elizabeth: Mrs. Rowe, I've been meaning to ask — how did you get on with those lettuce seeds I gave you?

Mrs. Rowe: Oh deary, deary me, Mrs. Blamey. I hardly like to tell 'ee. They plants came up lovely, big fat lettuces like you promised me, for I watered 'em every day and kept the slugs off 'em. But they was very bad eating, Mrs. Blamey?

Elizabeth: Were they? Whatever was wrong?

Mrs. Rowe: Well, I tried un boiled and they went to nawthing, tasteless they was. I tried a few leaves fried with my bacon — awful. And I tried stewing un with leg of beef — slimy they was. An' I tried baking them — hopeless. So thank you kindly for giving me the seeds, but lettuce is not to my taste.

Elizabeth: But you're not supposed to cook them, Mrs. Rowe.

Mrs. Rowe: *(amazed)* Not cook them? What do you mean?

Elizabeth: No, no. You eat 'em cut up raw, with your spring onions and a bit o' watercress.

Mrs. Rowe: Oh I don't hold with that nicky nacky stuff. T'ain't healthy not to cook your vegetables. You get caterpillars and all creeping 'bout your insides. Very sickly, you'll be, very sickly indeed, nigh unto death.

Exit Mrs. Rowe. Elizabeth returns to central area. Lights up centre. Ship sound resume. They all laugh.

Mary Ann: Tell us about they seeds again, Elizabeth. I do dearly like to hear about they.

Elizabeth: What again?

Mary Ann: 'Consider the lilies of the field' – the good book tells us to.

Elizabeth takes out an old newspaper cutting, various packets and calico bags of seed from her bag. They gather round – Keziah on edge of group.

Elizabeth: Did I show you the acorns?

Jane: *(ironically)* You did Elizabeth.

Elizabeth: Gathered these myself, I did, round October time, soon as I had the letter from my man saying as I must come out. A fine tree, that oak, growing in Mr. Trethewey's field. Strange to think of that oak's little ones growing up tall and strong on t'other side of the world.

Mary Ann: Large oaks from little acorns grow.

Keziah: You do say that every time, Mary Ann.

Elizabeth: And there's my vegetable seeds, all bought from Mr. Treseder's nursery down at Mylor. *(She takes the newspaper cutting and reads)*
Mylor Nursery, near Falmouth. J. Treseder begs to announce all the best varieties of kitchen-garden and flower seeds.
Intending emigrants supplied with good selections of Seeds of all descriptions, in convenient parcels, and carefully packed for voyages.

> *She rises and walks to stage R with her bag. Enter Mrs. Treseder with basket of seeds, to spot DR. Elizabeth joins her. Lights dimmed central area. Ship sound ceases.*

Elizabeth: Good morning Mrs. Treseder.

Mrs. Treseder: Good morning, Mrs. Blamey. *(She gives Elizabeth several packages).*

Elizabeth: That's my vegetables and flowers.

Mrs. Treseder: And have you thought of wheat and barley and potatoes?

Elizabeth: Perhaps I'd better have some wheat – not too much; they don't allow you much room on the ship, and my husband do say that he can buy some wheat and barley.

Mrs. Treseder: 'Tis an excellent strain though, Mr. Treseder says. *(Mrs. Treseder gives her more calico bags of seed).* There you are. Don't take 'em out mind. They're all packed for the voyage so the damp and rats an' all don't get at 'em. And 'ere's the bill. And may you have a safe voyage.

Elizabeth counts out money and gives it to her.

Elizabeth: Goodbye – and thank you.

Exit Mrs. Treseder. DR spot fade. Lights up centre. Elizabeth returns to central area.

Elizabeth: Did I tell you I saved some apple pips too? From our old Golden Pippin at home. I'm hoping they'll prosper.
Keziah: *(sniffing)* Mrs Lean, where I worked, said you never got nawthing good from apple pips. Fruit do taste of nawthing, she said – like eating straw.
Elizabeth: Well, well, I'll see. But I'm hopeful. There's young trees growing all around the village from pips off that tree and I've never had any complaints.
Mary Ann: The Lord will provide.
Keziah: Yes, but **what** will he provide? We don't really know, do us? Sometimes I feel sick with fright, wondering what New Zealand will be like.
Elizabeth: There's strange trees and plants, my husband says. Great ferns that hang down right over your head, and fruits such as we have never tasted – peaches, he do say, like those grown by Mr. Fox down Falmouth – my sister works in the house there, and she's seen 'un.
Mary Ann: Peaches? What manner of fruit are they?

Elizabeth: As big as an apple, but pink and gold and soft, my sister do say, - sweet and juicy with a big stone in the middle.

Keziah: Mmm!

Mary Ann: *(doubtful)* I don't know as I hold with eating they.

Keziah: God's fruits Mary Ann.

Jane: And what of the people? The native people – the Maoris? *(She kneels close to Mary Ann, teasing her.)* Just imagine – they live deep in the forests and creep out to attack the white man. And their faces. Think of their faces, Mary Ann – dark skins painted with streaks of white and red and blue – ready to POUNCE.

(Mary Ann shrieks. Keziah is muddled, fearful. Masks float dimly in the low light of the ship).

Elizabeth: For shame, Jane. Don't frighten the poor souls. My husband says you're quite safe when you're in the town or in the mission villages. For the Maori only stalks his forests and mountains and the gullies of his land.

Jane: Invisible in the sharp shadows of the ferns and of the trees they call the 'Tane Mahuta' – the God of the Forest – the great Kauri.

Keziah: Where the falls cascade into the bush fringed pools – there the Maoris roam. And strange birds sing.

Exeunt Masks. The ship lurches. Sound up briefly. Women stagger. Sound down to whisper.

Elizabeth: *(down to earth)* 'Tis true they resent the white man's coming. There'll be difficult times before we all live at peace. But many of them work with us, already, my husband says, in the docks and on the land.

Keziah: There's so much to fear. At least, at home, we knew where our troubles lay.

Mary Ann: *(whispering)* There's so many things I don't know.

Jane: We none of us know, Mary Ann. And surely the Lord will provide for you. You'll be met when we land by the people you're going to work for. You'll be whisked straight off to your new home. But Keziah and I must go to the immigrants' barracks, and find work as soon as we can. I'm sure we'll manage all right though. This time next year we'll all be truly settled. You'll be helping at the mission. Keziah and I will have found new work and prospects – and Elizabeth – why she'll be looking out on her garden patch watching for her seeds to come up.

Elizabeth: Yes – and there'll be my flower seeds – oh, where are they? I must have left them in my bag.

She searches with increasing alarm, in the holdall. She returns to the existing seeds, and searches through the packets. Then to the bag again.

Elizabeth: They're gone. I'm sure I put them in my bag. That's where I always keeps them, but they're not here now.

In panic she turns the bag upside down and searches through the contents.
Mary Ann joins in the search; Keziah searches also albeit half heartedly – Jane stands aloof. Whilst they are all occupied, Jane goes to Keziah's bag and

10

removes seeds. She puts them in her pocket and returns to her former position.

Jane: Here they are.

She holds the packets aloft. Varying reactions - Keziah for a moment astonished, then folds her arms and turns away - Elizabeth astonished. Mary Ann brandishes her Bible at Jane.

Mary Ann: Where were they?

Jane: Here, I have them here.

Mary Ann: You stole them didn't you? Creeping about at night. I know all about you Jane Gifford, and I know why you don't sleep. I wouldn't if I had done what you have done. You'm a wicked woman. I'm going to find the Matron and tell her what you done now. Thieving. There's no fear of God in you.

Elizabeth: No, Mary Ann. Wait. There's no need to bring Matron into this. We'll soon sort it out. You know if Matron gets to hear of it, there'll be enquiries made.

Mary Ann: Then all the more fool her for getting into trouble. *(She taps Bible)* "He that diggeth a pit shall fall into it." That's what it says - in Ecclesiclastix.

Mary Ann goes L, as if to the cabin door.

Elizabeth: Wait. Think Mary Ann. *(Stops her)* You'm one of us fortunate ones. Not everyone is as lucky as you - why, to go to work for people who was friends of your family - that's real security. Jane - and Keziah - have no such guarantee, and any hint of misdoing will ruin their chances.

Mary Ann: Well that's what I mean. Who would want someone who might thieve from them? It's only honest folk as is wanted in Auckland. In my opinion Jane should be sent back, on the first ship sailing to Cornwall, in chains. I heard what you done in Redruth, Jane Gifford, and shame on you.

Lights dimmed centre. Spot up Stage R. Sound ceases. Jane stands under R spot where she is joined by two witnesses, who stand each side of her. Jane has her back to audience. Witnesses face audience.

Witness 1: She worked at Wheal Harmony along of me and Mrs. Tregay there. *(She nods at witness)* It was about three months ago, may be four, as I do remember, the may was on the hedges, that she told me she was expecting. Go to the Union, Jane, I told her.

Witness 2: An' it was in September, your Honour, that I saw her coming home from work and she had something wrapped up in her apron, your Honour, and it was a little baby – dead. In Treleigh Lane it was, your Honour, near to Redruth.

Witnesses turn away. Jane faces audience.

Jane: I could go no further, your Honour, though I wanted to get home. I lay in the hedge, and the pain was – dreadful. I lost my senses, and when I came to again, I was lying on the baby. It was dead.

Jane turns her back to audience.   Witnesses face
audience again.

Witness 1: And she would not say the name of the father
your Honour, same as she don't tell you.
I told her that she must name the father, or she would be
sent to Bodmin.
Witness 2: *(sadly)* But four years in gaol is a long time, just
because you keep your silence.

Exeunt Witnesses U.R.   Jane returns to central area.
Dim out R spot.   Central lighting up.)

Elizabeth: And so, Mary Ann, I don't really think it
matters who did what, now I've got my seeds back —
they're all here — marigolds, pinks, my lavender and
wallflowers and forget-me-nots. I'll plant those little blue
ones to remember those at home. And pansies, little faces;
do you know, I'd forgotten I'd brought them.
Mary Ann: You may choose to forget, Elizabeth, but I
cannot. Jane must be punished. "Corrupt are they and have
done abominable iniquity." It do say so in the psalms, and I
shall go and tell Matron, so that the Commissioners shall
know what Jane has done.

She moves towards L as if to cabin door.   Suddenly
Keziah moves C.

Keziah: I stole them.

All except Jane look at her amazed — on Mary Ann's
face is disbelief.

Jane: Ssh, Keziah. Be quiet.

The ship lurches. Sound up briefly. Women stagger. Sound down to whisper. Jane pulls Keziah D.C. so that their conversation is almost private, away from the others.

Jane: Listen to me. I have nothing to lose. I've lived through the worst — *I know* the inside of Bodmin gaol. For four years. *(Pause.)* And I've never even begun to forget what I did to my baby. You'd think there'd be some sixth sense in a mother that would tell her when she was harming her little one, but there was no such sense in me. And Bodmin gaol did not 'expiate my sin', as Mary Ann would say. It is always with me. When I had the chance to come to New Zealand I thought I would put it all behind me. Perhaps in time I shall.
But you, Keziah, have a new life before you. And you have a good reputation.

Keziah sinks on to seat, Jane beside her.

Keziah: I know it was very wrong. I am sorry Elizabeth. *(pause)* My last mistress had a little flower patch till the cattle trampled it. It was the beautifullest thing I've ever seen. And when I saw your seeds I thought, 'Here's my chance to grow my own.'
Elizabeth: And so you shall, Keziah. But there was no need to steal them, you know. I'll give you some.

(Pause)

Mary Ann: *(suddenly and very loudly).* The Devil's own wickedness is abroad in this shop. It's not right, I tell you. They can't steal and get away with it. First Jane says she took them and now Keziah's confessing. It needs sorting out. They should be punished, both of them. "Let them be ashamed and confounded" – the psalm tells us. Jane is telling lies and so is Keziah.

Elizabeth: Be QUIET, you fool. You'll have Matron and the whole lot down on us.

Mary Ann: They will know for I will tell them. "God hath delivered me to the ungodly and into the hands of the wicked." They're telling lies. They will defile us all.

(She moves towards Jane, as if to hit her. Elizabeth grasps her hands).

Mary Ann: Let me go.

(She struggles uselessly. The bible falls to the ground. Jane picks the Bible up. Elizabeth releases Mary Ann's hands. Jane holds the bible above her head).

Mary Ann: Give that back to me. Now. It's mine. Give it back.

Jane: No. I'm tired of you quoting from your old bible. Aren't you Keziah?

Keziah Yes. *(She turns round to position herself behind Mary Ann. Jane faces Mary Ann).* Why's it called the good book? 'Tes all sin and misery.

Jane tosses the bible to Keziah, over Mary Ann's head. She jumps for it. Keziah throws it back to Jane.

15

They repeat the throwing, laughing and singing. The song grows increasingly raucous.)
Suddenly Mary Ann stops trying to catch the bible, her head is up as if listening. The movements of the other two cease. Spot up D.C. Mary Ann kneels in it. Lights dimmed central area. Enter Aunt Martha and Aunt Mag, standing either side of Mary Ann.

Aunt Martha: Have you learned your catechism, child?
Mary Ann: Very nearly, Aunt.
Aunt Mag: Psalm 60 "O God thou has cast us off" Do you have it by heart?
Mary Ann: I can't remember all the words.

(She crouches, warding off the voices.)

Mag and Martha: Learn, child.
Aunt Martha: *(Waving large key before Mary Ann's gaze).* If you don't know them by the time the church clock sounds, you'll be locked in the cellar, do you hear?
Mary Ann: No Aunt Martha. Please, please don't make me go in there.
Aunt Mag: God has no mercy on lazy little girls. *(Poking Mary Ann viciously with parasol).*
Aunt Martha: Girls who won't learn their catechism.
Aunt Mag: Too idle to learn their psalms. Yes, it'll be down the cellar again for you – no food.
Aunt Martha: No water. No light.
Mag and Martha: Till the wickedness is driven out of you.

(The two aunts nod at each other over their victim's head and exeunt).

16

D. Centre spot dimmed. Central area lights up. Sound returns – a whisper. Elizabeth walks D.S. to Mary Ann and helps her up.

Elizabeth: *(takes bible)* Come Mary Ann, take your bible.
Jane: Come and sit with us here, Mary Ann. We didn't mean no harm.
Keziah: We was only laughing at your funny ways of talking. I suppose we've all got our little quirks, and we've all had to learn to live with 'em, these past months.

They are all subdued and concerned by Mary Ann's bewildered expression.

Elizabeth: Take your bible and read it well, Mary Ann. The trouble is you've had too long to brood in these endless days, and you've tipped down the scales on the side of punishment for sin. But don't we read a lot of good things there, as well?
We must put away the memories of this night, my dears, though the past is always with us, remains a part of us. But now we must make new lives for ourselves. Just think what a chance we've been given, and we're all in the same boat.

Ship lurches. Sound up briefly. Women stagger. Sound down again to whisper.

Jane: Sinking
Keziah: Or swimming
Elizabeth: TOGETHER. For this is a time of hope and high expectation –

All face front, more formally. Throughout this speech the central lighting becomes brighter.

All, or severally: A time to sail from the old country and into the new – Planting the seeds sprung from Cornwall, tucking them into
The earth of our new land. Embracing all that is before us –
Not fearing the dangers and disasters that might come, but learning
From them. And one day our New Zealand descendants will
Revisit the old country, taking our new seeds with them
And planting them in the old earth, season and season about.

Blackout. Sound full volume for a few seconds, then fade.

The End

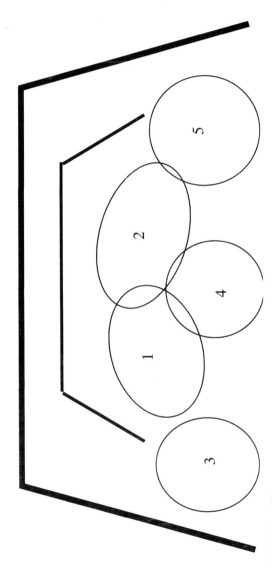

Lighting Note.

As the scene is in the stern section, below decks of a nineteenth century sailing ship, in the evening, the general lighting for the Centre Stage area is subdued.

In the original production, spots (1 and 2 on diagram) emphasized characters sitting on benches or standing around them.

Three areas (Down Left 5, Down Right 3, and Down Centre 4 on diagram) require occasional lighting – brighter than that of Stage Centre. These areas (3,4, and 5) should be dimmed out when not in use. They require hard edge spots. Lighting needs to be dimmed Stage Centre (1 and 2) when these spots are in use.

ABOUT THE PLAY:

Treseder's Seeds was presented by a group of members from four North Cornwall W.I.s at the 2001 National Federation of W.I.s' Drama Festival for Original Plays. There were 61 entries.
Treseder's Seeds won FIRST PLACE for both the Best Written Play, and the Outstanding Production.

ABOUT THE AUTHOR:

Christine Woolf, who lives in North Cornwall, has been involved in drama all her working life. She has written a number of plays, one act and full length, which have been presented by local amateur companies.